SO IT'S TIME... YOU ARE ABOUT TO EMBARK ON AN ADVENTURE!
YOU HAVE 5 MINUTES TO COMPLETE ALL 250 PROMPTS!
OKAY NO, YOU HAVE AS MUCH TIME AS YOU WANT.
BUT JUST THINK ABOUT WHAT YOU WILL BE ABLE TO ACHIEVE WITHIN THIS BOOK.

SOMEONE CAN IMPROVE SO MUCH WITH JUST 10 DRAWINGS, BUT HOW MUCH DO YOU THINK YOU COULD IMPROVE WITH 20 OR 100... OR 250!!!

OR MAYBE YOU'RE JUST LOOKING TO KILL SOME TIME AND DRAW SOME FUNNY THINGS! EITHER WAY, THIS IS GOING TO BE FUN!

LET'S GET GOING!!!!!

DRAW A CARTOON SELF PORTRAIT

Prompt 1:

Cows Abducting An Alien

Prompt 2:

A Cat Emperor

Prompt 3:

A Llama Assassin

Prompt 4

Squirrel Telling Ghost Stories Around A Fire

Prompt 5:

A Three Headed Necromancer

Prompt 6:

A Wiener-Dog With Bat Wings

Prompt 7:

Ninja Who Is Bad At Hiding

Prompt 8:

The Pumpkin King

Prompt 9:

Traveling Warrior With Tiny Legs

Prompt 10:

A Gnome With A Mohawk

Prompt 11:

A Robot Holding A "Free Hugs" Sign

Prompt 12:

A Fluffy Porcupine

Prompt 13:

An Actor Hiding From Fans

Prompt 14:

A Ninja With An Emoji Face

Prompt 15:

Evil Santa

Prompt 16:

A Dog On The Red Carpet

Prompt 17:

A Cop Who Hates Donuts

Prompt 18:

Evil Wizard Eating Breakfast

Prompt 19:

Hippie Rabbit

Prompt 20:

Your Best Friend As A Zombie

Prompt 21:

An Ice-cream Mountain

Prompt 22:

A Madhatter With A Battle-axe

Prompt 23:

A Dog Eating A Cheeseburger

Prompt 24:

Epic Valentines' Baby

Prompt 25:

A Floating Eyeball

Prompt 26:

Literally Raining Cats And Dogs

Prompt 27:

Scientist With Spoons and Forks For Limbs

Prompt 28:

An Elephant With A Huge Sword

Prompt 29:

A Frog With Lipstick

Prompt 30:

An Angry Raincloud

Prompt 31:

Undead Unicorn

Prompt 32:

A Pirate In A Dress

Prompt 33:

Hamburger Alien Saucer

Prompt 34:

A Robot Who Needs Glasses

Prompt 35:

5-Headed Chef

Prompt 36:

A Sad Monkey

Prompt 37:

The Wand Of Power

Prompt 38:

Bears Boxing

Prompt 39:

2 Monsters On A Date

Prompt 40:

A Fruit With Beautiful Hair

Prompt 41:

A Drooling Whale

Prompt 42:

Videogame Coming To Life

Prompt 43:

Grim Reaper Taking A Nap

Prompt 44:

Lightning Bolt Hugging Someone

Prompt 45:

Undead Car Tire

Prompt 46:

Werewolf Trying To Make Friends

Prompt 47:

Balloons Lifting A Horse

Prompt 48:

Vampire Rabbit

Prompt 49:

Man's Shadow Attacking Him

Prompt 50:

A Cowboy With A Jetpack

Prompt 51:

A Sloth Training For A Marathon

Prompt 52:

Garden Gnome On Airplane

Prompt 53:

A Dog Not Wanting Belly Rubs

Prompt 54:

A Crying zombie

Prompt 55:

Pizza Holding Pizza Cutters

Prompt 56:

A Buff Deer

Prompt 57:

A Taco Playing The Guitar

Prompt 58:

A Necromancer Hotdog

Prompt 59:

Kathulu Holding A Purse

Prompt 60:

Hovering Race Cars

Prompt 61:

A Doctor With A Blade Arm

Prompt 62:

An Innocent Witch

Prompt 63:

Alien Invasion

Prompt 64:

Plants Eating Another Plant

Prompt 65:

Undead Fairy

Prompt 66:

A Shark Lounging On The Beach

Prompt 67:

A Happy Banana

Prompt 68:

Goose Stampede

Prompt 69:

A Birthday Party Gone Wrong

Prompt 70:

A Sad Dinosaur

Prompt 71:

Yourself As A Superhero

Prompt 72:

Zombie Robot

Prompt 73:

A Gigantic Frog In The City

Prompt 74:

A Toxic Taco

Prompt 75:

A Skull Candle

Prompt 76:

A Witch Flying On A Giant Spoon

Prompt 77:

A Chicken With a Jetpack

Prompt 78:

A Marshmallow Climbing A Volcano

Prompt 79:

A Mermaid With A Laser Gun

Prompt 80:

A Cookie With Oversized Glasses

Prompt 81:

A Sick Queen Yelling At Jester

Prompt 82:

A Bird Who Drank Too Much Coffee

Prompt 83:

A Sidekick With A Wooden Sword

Prompt 84:

A Corgi Deepsea Diving

Prompt 85:

Vampire Brushing His Teeth

Prompt 86:

Your Teacher As A Zombie

Prompt 87:

A Frog Wearing A Mask

Prompt 88:

Goblins Mining Ice-Cream

Prompt 89:

A Strawberry On A Skateboard

Prompt 90:

A Basketball Player With Tiny Arms

Prompt 91:

A Giant Sleeping

Prompt 92:

A.I. Takeover

Prompt 93:

A Crying Otter

Prompt 94:

Vampire Pumpkin

Prompt 95:

A Girl Made Out Of Honey

Prompt 96:

Candy Corn Fighting A French Fry

Prompt 97:

A Robot Best Friend

Prompt 98:

A Pineapple Doing Pushups

Prompt 99:

An Evil Pencil Sharpener

Prompt 100:

Epic Little Red Riding Hood

Prompt 101:

Ground Hog Scared Of His Shadow

Prompt 102:

Space Pirates

Prompt 103:

A Shaman Summoning A Cake

Prompt 104:

A Lion With Evil Aura

Prompt 105:

Master Pumpkin Assassin

Prompt 106:

A Knight Riding A Dog

Prompt 107:

A Flower With A Knife

Prompt 108:

Ninjas Playing Pattycake

Prompt 109:

A Cake Monster

Prompt 110:

A Doctor Running From Apples

Prompt 111:

A Mummy Wrapped In Toilet Paper

Prompt 112:

Lollipop Garden

Prompt 113:

Robot Lifting Weights

Prompt 114:

Banana Showing Off His Boots

Prompt 115:

A Cat Baking A Cake

Prompt 116:

A Cute Goblin

Prompt 117:

A Bat Playing Hide And Seek

Prompt 118:

French Bread With A Mustache

Prompt 119:

A Kid Practicing Magic Tricks

Prompt 120:

A Potato Taking A Bath

Prompt 121:

A Pirate Knitting A Scarf

Prompt 122:

A Pig With A Top Hat

Prompt 123:

Cowboy Standoff With A Chicken

Prompt 124:

Peanut Butter & Jelly Sandwich Making Jam

Prompt 125:

Zombies At A Disco

Prompt 126:

Kid Sneaking Out A Window

Prompt 127:

A Robot With A Big Nose

Prompt 128:

Dog Sensei

Prompt 129:

Villain Pretending To Be A Hero

Prompt 130:

A Screaming Apple

Prompt 131:

Squirrels Spring Cleaning Their Tree

Prompt 132:

A Meteor With A Cape

Prompt 133:

A Zombie Wedding

Prompt 134:

A Cookie With Scary Teeth

Prompt 135:

A Toxic Rabbit

Prompt 136:

Gnomes Playing D&D

Prompt 137:

A Flower Smelling Another Flower

Prompt 138:

Astronaut Running Out of Food

Prompt 139:

Alien Driving A Convertible

Prompt 140:

A Disappointing Treasure Chest

Prompt 141:

Digital Pen Fighting A Pencil

Prompt 142:

Monster Hiding Under The Bed

Prompt 143:

A Squirrel With A Fancy Mustache

Prompt 144:

Sickly Old Swordsman

Prompt 145:

A Dog Burglar

Prompt 146:

Overly Fluffy Alien

Prompt 147:

A Bard Bugging An Adventurer

Prompt 148:

A Cute Bridge Troll

Prompt 149:

Eyeball With Feathers As Eyelashes

Prompt 150:

Lvl 1 vs lvl 100

Prompt 151:

A Dog Getting A Tattoo

Prompt 152:

Nerd Hitting On A Model

Prompt 153:

A Donut On An Adventure

Prompt 154:

An Evil Carnival Worker

Prompt 155:

A Titan Scared Of A Mouse

Prompt 156:

A Happy Ball Of Goo

Prompt 157:

Kid Giving Puppy Dog Eyes

Prompt 158:

Mouse Cutting Lion Nails

Prompt 159:

Alien Cowboy

Prompt 160:

A Barbarian With Wobbly Legs

Prompt 161:

A Goat Standing On Gravestone

Prompt 162:

Snowboarding Pig

Prompt 163:

A Headless Ghost

Prompt 164:

A Deer Selling A Car

Prompt 165:

Mom Catching A Falling Vase

Prompt 166:

A Monster Playing Video Games

Prompt 167:

An Evil Blacksmith

Prompt 168:

Pirate Dogs

Prompt 169:

A Potato Man

Prompt 170:

Aliens Selling Human Goods

Prompt 171:

A Fish In A Coffee Cup

Prompt 172:

A Cyborg Ninja

Prompt 173:

A Scared Ghost

Prompt 174:

Nerd Finding A Spell Book

Prompt 175:

Half Man Half Tree

Prompt 176:

Deactivating A Bomb

Prompt 177:

A Greek God Taking A Selfie

Prompt 178:

Candy Creature Invasion

Prompt 179:

A Roman Noodle Dragon

Prompt 180:

The Moon Screaming At A Wolf

Prompt 181:

A Rooster As A Superhero Sidekick

Prompt 182:

Villains In A Business Meeting

Prompt 183:

A Elf Surfing

Prompt 184:

The Dragon King

Prompt 185:

A Scottish Man Playing Golf With A Sword

Prompt 186:

A Panda Playing Drums

Prompt 187:

An Alien Sport

Prompt 188:

Why The Chicken Crossed The Road

Prompt 189:

A Madman Singing

Prompt 190:

A Polar Bear With Human Teeth

Prompt 191:

A Demon On Vacation

Prompt 192:

A Happy Star

Prompt 193:

Exploding Candy

Prompt 194:

A Ghost Controlling A Toaster

Prompt 195:

Baby Dragon Singing

Prompt 196:

A Clown Riding A Unicorn

Prompt 197:

A Stinky Art Teacher

Prompt 198:

Magic Turtle Healer

Prompt 199:

Warrior With 4 Arms

Prompt 200:

Epic Ms. Santa

Prompt 201:

A Rotten Breakfast

Prompt 202:

Massive Mosquito Monster

Prompt 203:

A Creepy Kid's Doll

Prompt 204:

A Barbarian Interviewing For A Job

Prompt 205:

A Corgi Cowboy

Prompt 206:

A Planet That's Alive

Prompt 207:

A Hero Sitting On A Rock

Prompt 208:

Creepy Living Clock

Prompt 209:

A Pirate On Vacation

Prompt 210:

Villager Doing A Handstand

Prompt 211:

Human Made Of Crystals

Prompt 212:

A Cute Robot

Prompt 213:

Lobsters Boiling Humans

Prompt 214:

Fighting Through A Blizzard

Prompt 215:

Monster Emerging From A TV

Prompt 216:

A Sneaky Koala Bear

Prompt 217:

Scared Kid In Graveyard

Prompt 218:

Evil Rollercoaster Cart

Prompt 219:

A Happy Skeleton Dog

Prompt 220:

A Ninja Spider

Prompt 221:

Monster Treasure Chest

Prompt 222:

A Witch With A Dumb Power

Prompt 223:

A Floating Castle

Prompt 224:

Scissors Running With Scissors

Prompt 225:

The Candy King

Prompt 226:

A Unicorn Superhero

Prompt 227:

Lightning Striking A Cow

Prompt 228:

A Man Stuck On A Tiny Island

Prompt 229:

Zombie Takeover

Prompt 230:

A Sad Swordsman

Prompt 231:

A Cactus With A Splinter

Prompt 232:

Adventurers Climbing Massive Mushrooms

Prompt 233:

Fire Breathing Mouse

Prompt 234:

An Astronaut Cow

Prompt 235:

Computer Overlord

Prompt 236:

A Man Falling Off Ship

Prompt 237:

Goblins Building A Rocket

Prompt 238:

Boss Battle On A Cliff

Prompt 239:

A Tiki Mask Eating Someone

Prompt 240:

A Carrot Wearing A Dress

Prompt 241:

The Sun And Moon Battling

Prompt 242:

Elf Making A Love Potion

Prompt 243:

Adventurer Find Magic Amulet

Prompt 244:

A Blind Bandit

Prompt 245:

Angel Scared Of A Baby Demon

Prompt 246:

Someone Sleeping On Cliffs Edge

Prompt 247:

Grim Reaper On A Magic Carpet

Prompt 248:

An Alien Dog With 4 Eyes

Prompt 249:

Happy Krampus

Prompt 250:

Giraffe Cop

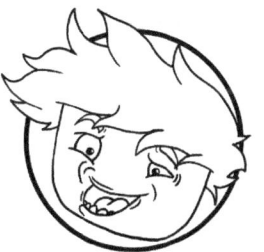

WELL YOU DID IT, YOU COMPLETED ALL OF THE PROMPTS IN THIS BOOK!!! WHETHER YOUR GOAL WAS TO IMPROVE YOUR DRAWING SKILLS OR IF YOU JUST NEEDED TO DESTROY SOME ARTIST BLOCK, YOU DID IT!

WITH THAT, I WOULD LOVE TO SEE YOUR WORK! MAKE SURE TO SHARE SOME, OR ALL OF YOUR WORK ON INSTAGRAM USING #NAUGHTYEGG250

I CANT WAIT TO SEE WHAT YOU MADE!!!